SOHO

RICHARD SCOTT

Soho

FABER & FABER

First published in 2018
by Faber & Faber Ltd
Bloomsbury House
74–77 Great Russell Street
London WC1B 3DA

Typeset by Hamish Ironside
Printed in England by Martins the Printers, Berwick-upon-Tweed

A CIP record for this book is available from the British Library

ISBN 978-0-571-33891-7

MIX
Paper from
responsible sources
FSC® C013254
www.fsc.org

4 6 8 10 9 7 5

For Daniel

Acknowledgements

Thank you to the editors of the following publications in which some of these poems first appeared: *Poetry Review*, *Poetry London*, *PN Review*, *Rialto*, *Swimmers*, *clinicpresents.com*, *Butcher's Dog*, *The Poetry of Sex* (Penguin, 2015) and *Wound* (Rialto, 2016).

Thank you also to the following writers for their words, queer theories and translations: Walt Whitman, David. M. Halperin, Valerie Traub, Sigmund Freud, Vatsyāyāna, Leo Bersani, Michel Foucault, Eve Kosofsky Sedgwick, Mark Doty, Socrates, Jean Genet, Rainer Maria Rilke, Ellis Hanson, Adam Philips, D. A. Powell, Felice Romani, Gerard Manley Hopkins, William Shakespeare, T. S. Eliot, Martin Sorrell, A. S. Kline, Norman Shapiro, Edmund White, Donald Revell, David Wojnarowicz, Henri Peyre, Stanley Burnshaw and Haydon Bridge.

Profound thanks to Matthew Hollis, Lavinia Singer and Hamish Ironside; and so much gratitude to Daljit Nagra and Edward Doegar for their unflinching belief in these poems.

Additional thanks are due to the Poetry Society, the Michael Marks Charitable Trust, the Arvon Foundation, Jerwood Charitable Foundation, Snape Maltings, the Poetry Trust, Poetry London, Harvard University's Center for Hellenic Studies, Goldsmiths College, the Faber Academy and the Rialto.

Loving thanks are due to my brother, sister, mother and father; and to Rhona Johnstone, Joan Scott and Margaret Theophanous.

Thanks also to Alice Dixon, Owen Willetts, Abigail Parry, Michael Mackmin, Chrissy Williams, Anna Selby, Reneé Doegar, Hannah Lowe, Rebecca Perry, Edwin Burdis, Liz Berry, Maura Dooley, Mike Sims, Sarah Macdonald, Jamie George, Elspeth Henderson, Matina Goga and Lina, Alex and Rafael Mahdavi for their support, encouragement and collaboration.

All the poems in this book are dedicated to my partner Daniel, who makes everything possible.

Contents

III   SHAME

IV   SOHO

SOHO

Public Library, 1998

In the library where there is not one gay poem,
not even Cavafy eyeing his grappa-sozzled lads – I
open again the Golden Treasury of Verse and write   COCK

in the margin. Ink stains my fingers. Words stretch to
diagrams, birth beards and thighs, shoulders, fourgies.
One biro-boy rubs his hard-on against the body of a

sonnet, another bares his hole beside some Larkin. A blue
sailor spooges over Canto XII. Then I see it – nestled like a
mushroom in moss, *tongue-true* and *vaunt* – a queer subtext

and my pen becomes an indigo highlighter inking up what
the editor could not, would not – *the violet hour* of these
men hidden deep within verse. I underline those that nature,

not the printer, had *prick'd out*; rimming each delicate
stanza in cerulean, illuminating the readers-to-come . . .

I ADMISSION

loose the stop from your throat . . .
WALT WHITMAN

le jardin secret

boys were my saplings
my whiff of green my sprouts
a hundred soft palms
reaching for my warmth
boys were my herbs
square-stemmed furred
scented with musk dank clove
& lovage boys were my
crops my ripe-red yield
my seeds each one exploding
onto my lips like sherbet
boys were my vines my
creepers my climbers
tattooing my neck back
& thighs with suckle boys
were my nettles my thistles
my thorns tickling me with
scratches & painting me
scarlet boys were my berries
my doll's eyes my yew
bitter on the tongue dizzying
& psychedelic boys were my
pitchers my fly-traps my
venus a petalled mouth wet
throat around a grave

crocodile

I know how I will die then
in a death roll scales to my
cheek claws sunk into my pale
shoulders water burning my
throat like whiskey the un-
countable rows of yellowed
teeth ringing my scalp and
in the heat of the thrashing
river he will press his white
rawness into me like that man
who held me from behind
when I didn't know sex and
gripped my mouth like a muzzle
and unsheathed his anger
stubble grazing my neck see
I have died already and somehow
survived hauled myself up from
the river mud to taste blue air
though I was not the same I
was carrion bleeding into the silt
and didn't I wear those wounds
well pity me the boy who cried
crocodile I have these moments when I
know I wanted it asked for it even
to be special to be scarred
wading along the riverbank feet
in the brown flow flirting with
wildness the green violence in the
shallows and I know he is swimming
back to me his horned body slipping

through sediment and weed for
nothing ever really heals he can
smell the red meat of me
bait lighting up the river

plug

remember when I ached to bottom be sub-
missive after a lifetime of playground fisticuffs and you
you urged patience bought me a valentine's day gift of moulded
silicone this marbled root which shone like a newly hatched
grub and glistened with spit when you put the tip into your mouth
and pressed its malleable girth against my hole
remember how I flinched and you bit my ear to distract me from
this muscular shuddering this movement of internal peony-dense
flesh this sting-twisting and somewhere near the centre of me I could
    feel a dilating
like how a sea-anemone releases its blood-rich tentacles into the
saline current remember how I came in your hand then external
symbol made fetish I tell you now I had been waiting
years to feel this brimming over this stoppered-up this
ripe fullness

four arias

after Vincenzo Bellini

Perduta, perduta io son!
    FELICE ROMANI

I don't remember when I lost it my
greenhorn my cherry my
only wedding satin is the
skin of my inside wrist thighs and

as far as lilies go I'm an arabesque
amaranthine puce scarlet etc
all those fancy names for red
that just mean red

you can be humble white
unopened but I tell you
we all bleed when it comes to it

you can sing of the april lily the
pearl the ice cave
but we all bud in muck and shit

♥

you're a little boy when you
sleep all curled up shrimp-
like your pillow-creased cheeks
dank brow and is it me you're
dreaming of eyelids caught
in birdlime clementine lips in a

mid-dream duet who is this
sound that comes to you in the
beetle-blue night an *O* a *B* a *V* perhaps
just never an *R* tell me his
name darling roll closer
sing it into the feathered pillow
so I might hold it against
your gorgeous mouth

♥

there you go again silver-
plating the bus stop
you make my veins pop blue
as a boy I could name all your waters

sea of crisis sea of cold you
did not turn away as I
jerked off explored my down with your
darling beam oh satellite

follow me home and I will open my
walls for you tonight I want
your lidless eye your pearly hum

wash my beard with translucence
transmute my skin to semi-precious metal
enter my mouth my anus with light

♥

lidl roses don't last
they rot
even a dash of 7up in the vase can't save them

the skin-pinks slacken scrotum-
like the reds
crumble to eczema scabs

I did not know you would fade so soon oh flower
and in the cemeteries
after pentecost

boys are heaping the
overblown fetid and sick into
wheelbarrows

scrubbing the gravestones with horsehair
wiping the lichen from your initials

Dancing Bear

Children bring me coins
to watch him balançoire, tombé –
they imagine he has a
forest inside, they close
their eyes to see him
foraging on a high cliff
above a burnished lake –
belly to the wet earth
but inside is just a savage
who loves with only his
claws, his wild mouth,
tears at honeyed flesh
with his barbed tongue
so I tamed him with
a rod, a crop, my fist –
starved him until he would
dance this way, that way.
At six o'clock you should
see me count my money –
hatfuls of brass and gold.
I uncouple his snout, rub
a drop of lotion in, pour
myself a drink as my
father unzips his bear skin –
places his naked head
on my lap – throat exposed.
He apologises to me
for all the places on my body
his hands have scarred
but I just close his eyes,

sing him to sleep,
nuzzle his ears – a blade
in my other hand.

Childhood

Can I come with you? asked the clown
in his caterpillar-green silk jumpsuit.

If you're going to say no then give me a crisp!
he spat, thrusting his fist spelt   L   O   V   E

into the open mouth of my Golden Wonder.
Crumbs stuck to his chapped lips.

I watched his grey beard struggle for freedom
under a smear of hastily applied pan-stick,

I counted the missing buttons on his coat,
the soup-stains on his ruff . . .

*Can I come with you or not, you little
tease?* His breath all salt and vinegar.

I nodded and gingerly led him home
by the path that winds through the cemetery.

Permissions

I am always writing my pamphlet of abuse poems   collecting rapey verse
like a tramp pocketing bin-butts   fuse 'em together later   have one mag-
nificent slow cigarette   and when my chap is read readers will   sharp
intake of breath   just as they do   mid-poetry-slam over a glass of house

red   white   pink whatever tickles your   how daring how dark what
marvellous images   the one about what was it the   schoolboy's sphincter
being like a   I never realised how pink   the inside   of a cheek
confessional   surely not this writer wasn't   that would be too awful

but how does one ask outright   my dear boy   is the I you well
I am not hinting anymore   please take your hand out of my trousers

'slavic boys will tell you'

slavic boys will tell you
when the chill of a journey sets in
simply upturn a chanced-upon mushroom
& taste the stem starting just above the dirty root-
pad – you must lick the length of it – dry out your tongue
on the spongy white limb & if it's spicy drop it – but if it's
salty, sweet or bland then eat especially if it's salty – eat
eat your fill
of the beautiful
firm growth
in your hand –
gorge on the
dense white
meat – eat, chew,
swallow hard – for
the forests are will-
ing to provide – stern,
cap & gills – they
know the hunger
of their men

Reportage

When I read how they poured petrol over that man
I see my own death in some outlying federal province.
Men I went to school with drag me into the arable scrub
chanting *queer!* in a different language – they slip off
my hood, wet my body with tractor fuel; the ringleader
spits in my face before pulling out his tarnished Zippo –
eyes skittering with white hate, his hand steady
and as if Europe were a funfair mirror I look back
across the thousand miles of moving corn, the brick-wall
estates, the shuttered-up villages – to see myself free,
pacing the avenues of a liberal city, scanning a tabloid –
poem forming in my head. We are not so different
that poor sod and I – I too was born into this world to have
dirt on my knees, another man's saliva in my mouth.

Sandcastles

A tall gent waits
inside the playground
not looking at any one

child but rather mostly
at the darkening door
of the public lavs

and the shadows
pooling within.

I wish I could enjoy
forging sandcastles with you
and your two-year-old,

filling the lime-green bucket,
packing it down
with the luminous shovel . . .

only now this man is
watching me –

he's caught me
among the families,
caught me trying to play daddy.

His gaze is iron-heavy
as he walks
to the lavatory door,

pauses
like he were crossing a road, enters . . .

In one version of the poem I
follow him in, slide up next
to the cistern. He bolts the grimy
cubicle door behind us. Un-

zips my jeans. In another I stay
building with your daughter,
perfecting the castle's invulnerable
keep. In another I am your

husband. I yearn to leave our
daughter alone for just a
handful of minutes and be loved,
in there, by him. In the last

version I am your daughter,
sculpting the intricate castle
from damp sand, oblivious to the
men, the poem being written.

cover-boys

top-shelf rags are not always pink curves&tits
sometimes an out-of-date *LATIN INCHES* hides
forgotten behind *RAZZLE* – three pixelated pricks
have stayed this hard since two thousand and five –
José Raúl Hotrod have stood inked jaw-locked
in a three-way french for some nine rugged years –
pecs still greasy tans Miami-orange fingers tucked
into each other's pits – interests include PS3 beer
skateboarding fisting being taken for expensive meals –
this is the future I wish for them – open-mouthed
wanton lithe&toned – instead of the all too real –
Wikipedia tells me Hotrod married a girl appalled
by his past – Raúl's serving time for battery in Bristol
Texas a born-again homophobe&José's heart exploded
on stage at Pride too much love or rather crystal

Fishmonger

Every Thursday he came to call
in his blood-licked surgeon's coat
and if my parents were out
I knew to order nothing but eggs
as his prices for fish were far too dear.

Once he took me into his van –
row upon row of gleaming flanks,
the rough brick-armour of crabs,
the stopped hearts of bivalves pickled in brine,
all resting on clouds of ice.

He let me douse his catch in ammonia
a secret to keep their sparkle, he said
and as I sprayed they spluttered
back to life – mouths gurning for water,
gills rippling like Venetian blinds,

coppers and silvers flashing and lathering.
I heard the mighty roar of the sea
surround his van like traffic.
He took me into his capable arms
so I would not cry out.

He fed me prawns to calm me,
wiped the brine from my lips –
let me try my first razor clam
unzipped from its pale hard shell,
the tip – soft and white and saline.

In that battered old Transit
I took the whole ocean into my mouth
and then he sent me home
with a dozen eggs –
so no one would be any the wiser.

Admission

he asks if my poems are authentic
do I have any experience in the matter
and by this he means abuse
and by this he means have I been a victim
I tell him the truth he talks to cover my silence
the Nigerian playwright who writes only
of the Second Liberian Civil War
how trauma is a shared thread
leading to other victims of molestation
how rape is a weapon blame

still in truth I wish he hadn't asked see I
want this man my friend to see me
as pure not in any way ruined or touched
dirty a tease a liar an attention seeker
he cites Wordsworth something familiar
about tranquillity and I want to ask
now that you know do you still like me
but like the boy when asked by his therapist
to say into the bathroom mirror
it's not your fault I remain dumb

museum

the unknown
sculptor chose his
marble well
birthing you
from a glittering
seam these flecks of
quartz pure light
illuminates your
chest it's late

afternoon the halls
are empty and I
am tracing a finger
across the hacks and
pocks these dis-
figurations of
time that tattoo
your torso oh my
kouros my apollo
you know first
hand only hand-
less the vulnerability of
queer bodies how the
earth does not value
us yet you have
survived de-
capitation the severing
of every limb part-
castration to be

here sun-
stroked hero of the
archaeological museum

I want to kiss your
sites of amputation
these rough-hewn
slices these weather-
ed absences I want to
run my tongue
along the lashed
small of your back
wet the hilt of your
battle-toned ass
so I do

bending my head
like a boyfriend
towards the reliquary
of your earth-
scarred sternum I
kiss your chiselled
flesh and find you
warm tasting of
sand and lime and
trace my tongue
down the line of
your groin towards your
injured sex

and there in the hall of
marbles I take you
into my mouth and
tongue your fractured
shaft the
ravaged break of
stone your
cut absence
has not damaged
your thrall if
this little of you is
beauty your entirety
must have been
blinding

for the longest
time people told me
I must change my life
but this is my life
this adoration of
men this worship of
those whom the
world has deemed
broken just as
you gave your
body to the earth
so have I given
mine to this echo-
ing voices and

I am already
steps away look-
ing back I can see only
the dazzling
slope of your cheeks
your sandstone
shoulder a
family surrounds you now
giggling pointing nodding
oh my unearthed
god they do not
understand you the
narrative of your body
how you bore the
darkness the years
of not being touched
your loneliness
which has been my
loneliness

Public Toilets in Regent's Park

The men here are bird-footed
feathering past the attendant's two-way mirror
unperturbed by the colonising micro-organisms –
bulleidia   cobetia   shigellosis

sliming across the yellowed groutings,
the fist-deep pool of brackish water
quivering in the U-bend, the tile that reads
for information on venereal disease telephone 01 . . .

All for the thrill of placing their knees
on the piss-stained cold, the iris shimmering
behind a hand-carved glory hole,
a beautiful cock unfolding like a swan's neck
from the Harris Tweed of a city gent's suit.

Whispers, gasps of contact echo
inside each nested cubicle! But careful –
the prying attendant will rattle
her bucket and mop if she spies four shoes!
Our men disperse as mallards from the face of a pond.

II VERLAINE IN SOHO

15 LOVE POEMS AFTER PAUL VERLAINE

What I'd give for a simple kind of affection . . .
(trans. MARTIN SORRELL)

blue-screen

your grindr profile is an emoticon paradise
where camels and kittens go
dancing and flashing but I can tell they are :-(
beneath their primary colours

your preferences brag in arial bold
SINGLE / PASSIVE / NO STRINGS FUN
but they don't like themselves
so melt back into the blue-screen

into the silent blue-screen blank and sad
that makes the emoticons dream within their
programming and code run like teardrops
C C++ sob beneath your touchscreen

love version of

tonight I watched you sleep
naked on the futon
face down sweaty like a small child
and knew that everything else was bullshit

it's so hard to stay alive these days
or sane
so keep on snoring danny
while I guard you like a rottweiler

being in love with you is fucking awful
cause one day you'll stop breathing
in this grey light you already look dead

but then you smile thank fuck
what are you dreaming about baby wake up
tell me if the word soul still means anything

tinder

blonde or brown-haired I swipe the screen
blue eyes
or green I swipe again looking for another
with a poet's eyes but a short back and sides

soft belly hard abs lean I swipe the screen
heart
desperate or damaged who cares so I
swipe again there's far too many of us

man-slut or boyfriend material left right
yes no
does it matter there's always another
each fitter than the last each newer

green

here's a plastic basket of polyester tulips
plus a heart-shaped card that sings I LOVE YOU
don't recycle them please
be happy with my pound-store presents

I stink I'm pretty sweaty I've been walking
this whole damp night to get here
let me curl around your converse cat-like
and dream of our cherry-days

maybe I could put my head still burning
from the memory of your hubba bubba kisses
onto your broad chest just till I feel a bit better
perhaps grab some shut-eye while you doze off

pastoral

above soho the sky
is super blue
bus minutes click down
MANBAR empties out

a fat pigeon burps
its coo of loneliness
shits
the sauna vents sigh

fuck me everything
seems so simple this early
suburbs boyfriends a-
sleep over the river

and you what have you done
standing there on a comedown crying
tell me how many men
came inside you last night

stupid love

violin music
hurts my gut
like a punch

I'm always
thinking about
what happened

then crying
wish I could
leave you

blow off
like an old
carrier bag

the hole

hope what is it be honest with me
you think it's desire a want
a wasp fizzing
for the gap in the window

are you sleeping at all
wine helps whiskey too
I haven't gone to bed sober for eleven years
I don't know any lullabies

tell me to fuck off
if you want sympathy is so pat
you just want him back him

walking through your brain neck
still smelling of davidoff cool water
that wasp is always thinking of the rose outside

what kind of slob leaves a used mattress
on the street tide-marked with
sweat piss blood and is that maybe cum
I swear you can see his outline in bodily fluids

and he's not alone
four knees four palms four buttocks tattoo
the damp quilted magnolia cotton
they sure had a happy horny time of it

so what happened
did they move to hastings or get a swanky new one
the dfs memory foam 900

or did all that sex turn into regret
I know something about regret I've been
chucked away often covered in hickeys sex-bruises

like to go for long walks

I was always bimbling about KT3 SW20
looking down each suffocating avenue
for someone just like me

every driveway park bench
each public lavatory
was an X might mark the spot

remember those pre-grindr days
when loneliness stung like a hunger
and you wanted to give yourself away like a milk tooth

homo do you still walk until your shins ache
up turnpikes across spaghetti junctions
through industrial estates along the towpath

your only treasure map
the salt-flesh wall in your stomach your semi

heath

the moon bleeds
light onto the black ash
every branch
in this dismal canopy
rasps indifference

like an ex-boyfriend

the salt marsh
is full of drowned things
the walnut trees
beckon like trade
the dark moves

no you are not dreaming

this desperate place
this scrub
cold
as dead starlight
violet

is your home now

the presence of x

you believe in magpies
one for sorrow two for joy
I think that's lame

you believe in disney films
aurora ariel belle get their prince
I think that's heteronormative bullshit

you believe in reincarnation
motivational speakers crystals runestones
I think that's super annoying

I believe in sex the blue hours
you've spent fucking me
the bruises you left on my arms

I'm the monk and you're stigmata
only this isn't some straight to dvd thriller
starring christian slater and donnie wahlberg

today

memories what the fuck do you want
making a fat pigeon beat the air again
the copper sun roll back years
the yellowed woods chatter with decay

we were alone together him and me
drunk sad our thoughts coming down
he turned his black look my way said
is this happiness his voice metallic

his voice which had been so green
like my mouth my body
how I kissed his peachy neck and thighs

yeah the first years are so ripe
when open-mouthed kisses fill the silence
that today is long

sertraline 50 mg

it's raining in my heart
what does that even mean and
why am I so sad
all the fucking time
still it pours on
the slate roofs are black
the gardens a swamp
droplets on the pavement
such white noise is
almost calming so
how come my head's a cloud and
my heart's a puddle
middle class boys like me
haven't known tragedy
and yet this dark rain
saturating my heart

in the style of richard scott

my moon is a man
he's watched me get naked in parks cemeteries by the canal etc
the other stars belt spade massive crab
are pretty meaningless and dead anyway

there's no more music in poetry
than in my boyfriend's whispered voice
both make my heart pump
belly spasm

I don't forgive you bullies exes
the man who punched me the one who touched me
but I love my dad
even though he did and said shit shit things

I am free now still
it hurts everyday so I read
mark and walt and arthur and constantine and gregory and thom
    and my boy paul
write poem after poem about

other people's dreams are boring

I dreamt I was at CHARIOTS last night and
two lads
one blue-eyed one black
slipped out of the bleach-stinking steam

you should have seen their towels
damp with sweat hugging their smooth waists
smothering thighs flanks
cupping the dangerous meat between their hips

they pulled me into their labyrinth of clouds
terrycloth swaying like silk ball gowns
on some itv drama about adultery or longing and

there in the wet room tiled like an abattoir
these boys opened their towels like the velvet curtains
    at an opera house
and I opened my mouth to sing

III SHAME

Shame, too, makes identity.
EVE KOSOFSKY SEDGWICK

[have rubbed myself against bark]

have rubbed myself against bark
to feel a touch different from my mother's

filled my mouth with soil for a kiss
pulled the buds from an upright shoot

shoved my shorts down and sitting
pierced by the wilderness

face wet with want
felt loved

which is another boy's
torture and

the sky was pixelated tv
and shame

scabbed my lips
shut

[mostly because I had been re-reading freud]

mostly because I had been re-reading freud
paraphrased by bersani *the finding of an*
object is in fact a re-finding of it when you   Freud/Bersani
spanked me six seven times before penetration I
thought about dad whacking my thighs for drinking
bleach that one hot summer in new malden
nestled towards the back of the shed beside a
mallet cloudy like lemonade it didn't burn
exactly but felt wrong in my mouth like
bone so I yelled for help which was two dad
fingers rammed down my throat chunder
then the open fist *the one who protects the*
one who tends who was gentler I wonder both   Freud/Bersani
bearded chests lightly furred like weasels

[even if you fuck me all vanilla in]

even if you fuck me all vanilla in
out slow responsible vaguely tender
it's still not regular intercourse

even if we're missionary the hairless
backs of my knees against your shoulders
it's still an act of protest even if I'm

moaning at a respectful volume
even if you're wearing an extra-strong
condom even if I make you cum

on my thigh not inside even if I
fall in love as you pull out flop over
it's all still a middle finger up flaming

rag stuffed into napalm revolution fuck-
ing anarchy we are still dangerous faggots

[you slug me and]

you slug me and
just for a second I forget how pathetic I am
lips all prickle fizz of blood

those middle-range pleasures that make up everyday life
are nothing for me   Foucault

find me in solitary a rose
garden of bruises

fist flat of the palm back of the hand hollow hand   Vatsyāyāna

these are your tools my
limit-experiences

I need you to be my black-site interrogator
ask the terrible questions of my flesh

unearth the nail-bomb of my heart
beat the queer into me into me

[no muscular fields just scrub and]

no muscular fields just scrub and
butcher-boy works a zero-hours contract
at romford meats ltd

glittering knife ebayed he
wields a chainsaw to halve
the ruddy carcases the

very air is close with proteins and
on his lips offal-
flecks bone-shards

there is that in me
I do not know what it is
but I know it is in me   Whitman

and he cannot cut it out
it needs to be fed

[under neon lights my arms glow scar-]

under neon lights my arms glow scar-
tissue crescent-moon weals these
healed but not forgotten medals of a
childhood trend to grab wrists forearms
on the playground and clasp down
dig nails in for the squeal and blood I
can't say I didn't like it though this
touching this sticky wince the twist of
flesh the fresh wounds smiling up at
me these days I wear my scars like a
bandana to mark my preference my
fetish they read take me home rake
your nails across my body make me
feel like a kid again make me bleed

[but our crab shells are orange]

but our crab shells are orange
barnacled strung with sea grass

in them I cannot see heaven just
the tanned forearms creamy skin of

every boy whose thigh I licked before throat-
ing their cock men change when you do this

reek of power want to jam your head down
gag you *not so bad to die* like this maybe   Doty

maybe and the grey sand rimed with oil
diesel rainbows is littered with death

so many exoskeletons glinting at dusk like
sweat beads on a man's body as he bucks and

cums and mark says *we cannot know*   Doty
but I know that sex will kill us all

[5am cadaver-slack in my arms]

5am cadaver-slack in my arms
I've no clue what
you're thinking

there are limits to me limits
to my understanding terms like

spiritually liquefying speech
love   Bersani
slip by me

still this one reverberates like
a wasp in a paper cup

the boy is in love but he has no idea of what he loves   Socrates

none of us have ever known what we're doing
homos each one of us opaque as rose
quartz I am so lost

[legs straight as you go forward knees]

legs straight as you go forward knees
bent to pick up speed all those times you
swung so high and thought the taut chain
might buckle and the green park was a paint
smear and each lungful of blue air ozone oh
you didn't need a push could do this all on your
own the backs of your knees bruised scabby
and still this feeling uncanny weightlessness
upon walking into the bathhouse each half-
smile nod sneer pushing you further into the
steam maze until you come to a man prostrate
waiting for you and something like vertigo
pushes you onto him inside him and you
move fast and rough like a kid on a swing

[are you looking for me in these lines]

are you looking for me in these lines
like a urologist examines piss for blood

come sit with me
and I will tell you all the truth I have left

how touch is everything and
underneath sex is your beginning

pick up the glass shard the bent paper clip the razor and
dig with me for more answers

I too am not a bit tamed
I too am untranslatable   Whitman

by now you should know that
shame is cellular real

as the shiny blood drop rising ripe
calamus root sweet flag on your inner thigh

[how could I forget the hot-faced]

how could I forget the hot-faced
trauma the instant rash-jam that spread a

sunburn across my face neck ears
ages nine to twenty-two when a boy

looked at me or looked away my blush
we called it except for dad who said

what family are you a member of
but shame is my birthmark semaphore

of blood vessels skin-stain *a shame-
prone person is a person who has been*

shamed says eve still I don't remember   Sedgwick
the stone just the ripple-flash of heat-

pricks moving *from shame to shyness*
to shining I hated still hate this body   Sedgwick

[people say shit like *it gets better*]

people say shit like *it gets better*
but what they mean is *there'll always be haters*
only you'll be older

you are twenty-seven when your father says

gay people die of terrible diseases

you are twenty-eight when a poet says

makes for uncomfortable reading

you are thirty-one when your father says

don't tell anyone you're my son

you are thirty-five when a poet you love writes

that's so gay

the world has given you a silk rose
dyed all the colours of sunset a polystyrene
peach love I mean shame

[you spit in my mouth and I]

you spit in my mouth and I
taste petals was always a

sensitive boy and really what's
changed the rose garden at

two am *here I shade and
hide my thoughts* flowers   Whitman

close in on themselves like
fists and men are walking

beneath the vines tell me how to
celebrate myself twenty years of   Whitman

feeling for body parts in the soil-
scented dark and all I have learned

the opposite of shame is not pride

[shame on you faggot for bending whitman to your will co-]

shame on you faggot for bending whitman to your will co-
opting him into your self-help circle-
jerk willing him to yawp across the tattered ages just for you
when you aren't even his type he liked them younger
hopeful and all those other theorists what did you think
leo
    paul
        mark
            jean
                eve
                    michel would be your fore-
faggots signpost your backdoor out of shame shame
on you faggot and shame on me an italicised quote is no talisman
all this must be lived through a second puberty this burning

(. . . and if I can just push through this decades-long blush this
SHAME SHAME SHAMEFULNESS
will there be something waiting for me

a distillation of self a
queer beauty

purer than memory certain un-
flinching wide-eyed

a fabulous transcendence . . .

and in the deepest offal-shadowed parts of myself I feel the
thought of myself

free from shame but made from shame

*. . . is shame to be valued only at the moment one no longer
feels its inflammation*   Hanson

no shame is your gift from the world to the
world that fucked still fucks you)

[I am the homosexual you]

I am the homosexual you
cannot be proud of

turbulent fleshy sensual breeding   Whitman

I am the boy your
father would beat
or fuck

I spent my formative years
at urinals
defacing the grout

WILLINGMOUTH

my scraping like a boar's tusk on bark
piercing through the world's contempt   Genet

I am not toxic am residual   Sedgwick

IV SOHO

Oh My Soho!

for Daljit Nagra

All this I swallow, it tastes good, I like it well, it becomes mine . . .
WALT WHITMAN

I

Urine-lashed maze of cobble and hay-brick! Oh
chunder-fugged, rosy-lit, cliché-worthy quadrant. I
could not call you beauteous but nightly I've strolled your
Shaftesbury slums for a bout of wink and fumble.

Or hopped the iron-wrought gates of Soho Square, dank-
scented potagerie, to harvest night-blooming buds under ripening
street lamps. Or sloped to the Broadwick bog-house
where the cisterns trickle in harmony like the three-stringed lyre,

where the glory holes flicker pink-tongued. Or jumped the queue for
MANBAR video bar, sweaty fluoro-phoenix risen from the
foundations of MARGARET CLAP'S molly house. All this in lithe
Eros' crosshairs, queer angel atop the meat-rack of

Cleveland Street. Eros wants me cum-crazy, boshed on lust,
but I need a clear head for this trip. I am to be homo-historian –
mean to turn Biogrope to biography, foreskin to forbearer.
    Oh my Soho,
let me linger out tonight. I have rainbow warriors to exhume . . .

So who first kilned the homo holy grail? Was it the hunky
Spartans, those man-on-man love missionaries who queered our
leafy Roman-outpost? Or did changeling Jove himself,
　　god-talons
sharp for boy-flesh, his comely-white feathers, fashion our same-

sex revolution? Was Soho still Fleet-pasture then? Ganymede
dozing on his crook, horned goats swelling the coppery paths?
And who might we salute for imported whips, banishment, sober
　　castration,
point-and-stare-in-the-marketplace marble-heavy shame?

See, for a man to pierce a man with anything more than just a dick,
　　e.g. *AMARE*,
was patheticus. Even Hadrian's bust-worthy boyf, Antinous,
dredged sopping from the Nile, reborn a pink-dwarf constellation,
suffered his queer temples to be sacked and plundered

at the hands of Constantine's Christian gentrification. And didn't
Caesar's bullying become blueprint for our own colonisations?
Filching glittering hoards of conflict minerals, leaving our subjects
　　with leather-
bound copies of Leviticus. Centuries of sodomites caged for what?

An aqueduct, Regency marble? And didn't we learn the consul's trick
of bread, circuses, the gruff gladiators' bloodstained six-pack?
Still, what is Rome tonight to the t-shirted ladz bumming menthols in
    the disco line
other than *Caecilius est in horto*? Other than an HBO box set?

III

Silver-crowning Soho, throbbing within the white marble halls
of our British Museum, is the Warren Cup. That
Uranian chalice of Victorian naivety. That blueprint of queer
hope. Smithed when Roman homos would meet in

secret. Unearthed, buffed-up when us homos would still meet in
secret yet worshipped by Warren's velveted posse as a
symbol of freedom and reimagined, fetishised as forward-thinking!
Still there is more to queerness than just trans-historical

bum-fun. More than the cup's glittering nostalgia of myrtle wreath and
leather strap, of embossed bearded boy-love, of gilded lithe limbs.
What about the modern homosexual's plea for lifestyle, joint-
lodgings, legality? What about love? Oh my Soho, Warren's

cup is no wedding cup but a how-to-fuck cup passed around at toga'd
orgies. A mischievous relic. Every empire, ours included,
has done its savage best to stamp us out, redact our mission – its
violent reception from the permanent collection.

Oh my Soho, you are my museum tonight! Show me instead our true
lineage. Show me the off-stage trauma, the sentences for
sterile acts, the gleaming shears, the specific dismemberments, the
smouldering pyres. Show me the Poland Street pillory,

where even in Warren's faux-progressive epoch, boys would hang
their blue-eyed heads in shame – all now just pissed-on tarmac.
Oh my Soho, recall for me the WHITE SWAN twenty-seven. Hauled
     from ale-
soaked interiors into the frowning dawn, paraded by the Peel

Street Runners as dangerous poofs! My brothers, may I call you
brothers? The billowing rainbows of Beak Street still mark
our gallows road. Tyburn tree casts a lengthy phallic shadow over
Soho tonight. Look up to watch the queer fruit hang, swing!

And what of the fifty-seven silent martyrs, names blotted from the
ledger in the reign of bloody Victoria? What of gay king Eddie
pokered by his own desire? What of horny Henry's bloodthirsty
Buggerie Acte? What of enforced penance, of

breaking rocks, of the sharpened Judas Cradle? Oh my Soho,
my tongue's untied by trauma! We're a people robbed of
ancestors – they were stolen, hooded, from us. We're born of
citizens yet penned in our prime postcode under pix-

elated surveillance. Surrounded by smiling agent provocateurs,
plain-clothed pretty coppers at the pissoirs, gangs of aggro
potent lads, the bisexual terrorist – his bag-blast of nails.
Oh my Soho, my haven, my bunker, my West Central

Bank, take me back to the black vaults of Heaven where the medieval
leather daddies shine like ripe aubergines and I can
slow dance with martyrs under strobe. Within the popper-fog
their scarred bodies jolt like illuminated script.

v

Before Sunday jazz at COMPTONS was the sickly SWISS TAVERN.
Its bruise-dark windows, boisterous backroom, posters of
symptoms bearing photocopied lesions – the Rorschach of K.S. and the
new scare-lingo PCP, LAV, GRID. So is illness our ancestor?

And how many times have I queued for a prick in the shadow of
    SUBWAY, sub-
woofing birthplace of the UK virus, to feel made *clean*? I have
touched genocide with my tongue again and again and somehow
learnt nothing but fear. And how many of us wasted on

AZT, on silence, on blood-hysteria before express clinics set up their
lunch-hour prick 'n' go's, before Truvada-whore became a hashtag?
Oh how far we've come since the silver nose of syphilis, since the Santa
Maria's cargo'd gonorrhoea! Oh my Soho,

just how did our gorgeous species survive the Parliamentarian's
      drug-embargoing
slaughter? The proxy-diagnosis? The segregated blood-drives?
The censored sex-ed classes? The NHS's test and detain orders?
The government's waning funds? The GP's apathy? Ignorance.

VI

These days we homos are held under glass while the warm geneticist
prods at our nature. Are we nothing more than chemical
enzymes? Rainbowed dots dividing under the sanitised glare
      of 4×, 10×, 40×?
Behold chromosome marker Xq28, our root, our cocky code

shining on a slide like the rosy hues of St Bartholomew's stained-glass
      flayed chest –
scarlet, fuchsia, carmine – patinating the Rupert
Street pavements. And always a young homo sloping by, scratching at
scabs, spots, scars – piecing together last night's happy hour,

the beer-blur of boys, the what-went-where, the who-did-what-to-me?
Oh my Soho, my teaming Petri dish, my ER, my graveyard!
So many of us born at the foot of that televised tombstone. So many
      faggy-
foundlings orphaned on your gum-pitted kerbs.

Oh My *SO HO!* For centuries your name meant kill the animal, the
    heretic, the
revolutionary. And yet no one is screaming – we are dancing through
    the slaughter
as your name pulses from within the bass. An epigenetic
earworm. An open wound. And Quentin's beloved

BLACK CAT, Oscar's KETTNER'S, the CARAVAN CLUB and
    GOLDEN CALF
are razed – rebranded gastro-pubs to serve reclaimed chitterlings,
    sweetbreads, faggots –
are pre-fab condos with plate-glass views, are PRET A MANGERS.
Even viral SUBWAY has been bricked-up, vaccinated!

We, too, are not immune to this shameful progress; us homos are no
    longer revolting!
Too busy sending dick pics and I saw Saint Peter Tatchell shirtless,
    bruised under L.E.D.s
at G-A-Y. Colours moved across his scarred chest like jellyfish stingers
as he dreamed of his bisexual future, his post-homophobic Elysium.

VIII

But how many brothers sat in stripes after the celebrated law change?
    Sodomy,
our lusty labour of love, was a pastime only for those with
domestic privacy – doors, walls, curtains – but what if Soho was your
house? And how did they feed us this hoax of legality

when thousands of comrades still throng the sex-offenders register?
    Cottaging,
cruising, innocent importuning – even open-mouthed
kissing sent us to the dock, postured in shame. Oh my Soho, your
neon labyrinth became our plain-sight priest-hole.

And who were these sheathed men – helmeted, rubber-gloved –
    raiding bars,
saunas, WCs – our disorderly houses enema'd one by one?
Even holding hands could mean, can still mean, a hospital visit –
body in splints. And who am I to write 'us'? Legal

ever since I was born – *POOF, FAG, BUM-CHUM, FUDGE-PACKER,*
the occasional fist – my *only* hard labours. Such
ripe fanfares for a boy-deviant, a back-row punching bag in the
biology lab when Section 28 was making us sick, sicker.

Oh my Soho, am I being ungrateful? All this almost progress –
    2017 and
we've zipped from mental illness to supposed equal
in only one hundred and forty-seven years. Contrary sexual
    sensationalists
to citizens worthy of a lifestyle. But did we down our placards

for the sake of a good party, our very own GHETTO? Oh my Soho,
spin me back to your parades, your protests, your pride –
when a rainbow flag was a sigil and a cocktail was flaming!
    Oh my Soho,
was there ever an invulnerable queer body?

IX

Oh my Soho, my omphalos is your plague-pit of cross-rail diggings,
    the bleach-
stink of your newly rinsed tarmac, your 2for1 WKD deals,
your tatty rainbow flags, your porn shops, your cottages!
Warren's cup transforms from dirty secret to prize exhibit but I

am like you my Soho. I'm chock-full of shame, riven with dark man-
jostling alleyways, a treasure map of buried trauma. In you
I have spent my life – drunk, poppered up, tarnished, tear-stained,
    corroded, Eros-
like. Oh my Soho, unfurl the chiselled leaves of my fruit

family tree. Give me my batty-birth rite. Baptise me with pigeon
shit, cheap lager, cum. Oh my Soho, my urinal'd
utopia, my Mary-Jerusalem, my homo-land – may I call you my
daddy? You teach this queer continuation on the breaking

wheel of pansy progress so I still take my body into dungeons,
    cubicles, alleyways –
flesh to the grindstone – my only weapon against normativity!
    Oh my Soho,
your hunting cry rallies within my hot-pink veins. Familial
voice calling us home to reseed History.